TECHNICAL REPORT

9 to 5: Do You Know If Your Boss Knows Where You Are?

Case Studies of Radio Frequency Identification Usage in the Workplace

Edward Balkovich, Tora K. Bikson, Gordon Bitko

Approved for public release; distribution unlimited

RAND INFRASTRUCTURE, SAFETY, AND ENVIRONMENT

The research described in this report results from the RAND Corporation's continuing program of self-initiated research. Support for such research is provided, in part, by donors and by the independent research and development provisions of RAND's contracts for the operation of its U.S. Department of Defense federally funded research and development centers.

Library of Congress Cataloging-in-Publication Data

Balkovich, Edward.
    9 to 5 : do you know if your boss knows where you are? : case studies of radio frequency indentification usage in the workplace / Edward Balkovich, Tora K. Bikson, Gordon Bitko.
      p. cm.
    "TR-197."
    Includes bibliographical references.
    ISBN 0-8330-3719-6 (pbk. : alk. paper)
    1. Electronic monitoring in the workplace—United States. 2. Radio frequency—identification. 3. Radio frequency identification systems—United States. 4. Employee rights—United States. 5. Privacy, Right of—United States. I. Title: Nine to five. II. Title: Radio frequency identification usage in the workplace. III. Bikson, Tora K., 1940– IV. Bitko, Gordon. V. Title.

HF5549.5.E37B35 2005
331.25'98—dc22

2004027392

The RAND Corporation is a nonprofit research organization providing objective analysis and effective solutions that address the challenges facing the public and private sectors around the world. RAND's publications do not necessarily reflect the opinions of its research clients and sponsors.

RAND® is a registered trademark.

© Copyright 2005 RAND Corporation

All rights reserved. No part of this book may be reproduced in any form by any electronic or mechanical means (including photocopying, recording, or information storage and retrieval) without permission in writing from RAND.

Published 2005 by the RAND Corporation
1776 Main Street, P.O. Box 2138, Santa Monica, CA 90407-2138
1200 South Hayes Street, Arlington, VA 22202-5050
201 North Craig Street, Suite 202, Pittsburgh, PA 15213-1516
RAND URL: http://www.rand.org/
To order RAND documents or to obtain additional information, contact
Distribution Services: Telephone: (310) 451-7002;
Fax: (310) 451-6915; Email: order@rand.org

Preface

Radio Frequency Identification (RFID) tags are finding their way into a broad range of new applications that have raised concerns about privacy. There is little to inform the calls for a national debate and the legislative proposals that have resulted. The concerns expressed demonstrate how emerging information technologies can upset the balance of privacy, personal benefits, and public safety and security. Although proposed retail uses are new, RFID tags have been used to control access in the workplace for over a decade. We became interested in how existing workplace policies might serve to inform a larger debate about how to weigh competing needs when new technologies or new uses disturb existing balances. We undertook a replicated case study of six enterprises to understand their policies for collecting, retaining, and using records obtained by sensing RFID-based access cards. We found that the workplace policies we surfaced share a number of common features (data are used for more than access control, access control system records are linked with other enterprise databases, and security and employment practices trump privacy concerns) and that these policies are not communicated to employees.

This report results from the RAND Corporation's continuing program of self-initiated research. Support for such research is provided, in part, by donors and by the independent research and development provisions of RAND's contracts for the operation of its U.S. Department of Defense federally funded research and development centers.

Contents

Preface...iii

Figure and Tables vii

CHAPTER ONE

Introduction 1

CHAPTER TWO

Privacy in the Workplace...5

CHAPTER THREE

Methods...7

CHAPTER FOUR

What We Found 9

Architecture of the RFID Systems Studied...9

Responses to Interview Questions 10

CHAPTER FIVE

Results 15

CHAPTER SIX

Discussion..17

Recommendations 17

Reality Versus Recommendations 19

Conclusions 20

Appendix: Interview Questions 23

References..27

Figure and Tables

Figure

1. Elements of a Typical RFID Access Control System 10

Tables

1. RFID Access Control System Characteristics 11
2. Users and Uses of the RFID Access Control System Data.. 12
3. Policies Related to RFID Access Control System Data 13

CHAPTER ONE

Introduction

New information technologies have created unprecedented opportunities to collect, store, and transfer information. Technology can be applied to make our lives both easier and safer, but it can also diminish our privacy and civil liberties. Effective decisionmaking about relationships among personal convenience, public safety, security, and privacy requires many kinds of knowledge. Together with Carnegie Mellon University, we outlined an empirical approach to generating such knowledge (Balkovich et al., 2004).

As a starting point, RAND examined a commonly used information technology—Radio Frequency Identification (RFID) tags in access cards. Access cards are often used in the workplace to control entry to facilities. Data describing a card's use by an individual employee can be collected by an access control system and analyzed. This common deployment of RFID technology should require policies to balance the concerns of personal convenience, security, and privacy when access cards are used. This report examines such contemporary workplace policies.

RFID technology is on a path that promises to make it a pervasive technology (Covert, 2004). There are high-profile private- and public-sector commitments to its use in tagging and tracking objects (Feder, 2003; Henry, 2003). These commitments are based on the perceived benefits of the technology. Those benefits include improvements in logistics, supply chain management, and retail sales (*RFID Journal*, 2002a, 2002b; "About EPCGlobal Inc.," 2003). They also include security applications such as that of the Mexican federal judiciary (Weissert, 2004) and proposed improvements to patient management in hospitals (Schwartz, 2004).

These perceived benefits must be balanced against concerns about privacy. Proposed retail uses of RFID tags have generated some of the greatest concerns (see, e.g., Albrecht, 2002, 2003). Such concerns about potential abuses of the technology have, in turn, spurred legislative proposals to limit its use in California, Missouri, Utah, Massachusetts, Maryland, and Virginia[1] as well as calls for a national policy discussion (Leahy, 2004). This privacy debate is primarily about a use of RFID technology—retail sales—that is yet to be deployed, let alone understood.

Although RFID technology is far from being as pervasive as retail sales might eventually make it, it is already in widespread use in workplace access cards. We hope to inform the debate about future uses by studying the policies and behaviors in existing uses. In this re-

---

[1] A summary of proposed state legislation can be found in "2004 RFID Legislation," 2004.

port, we examine these policies from the perspective of organizations using RFID-based systems to control access to their facilities.

To be sure, differences exist between RFID in tags for objects and RFID in access cards. The use of RFID in access cards, credit cards (e.g., Exxon Mobil Oil Corporation, 2003), and toll tags (e.g., New Jersey Department of Transportation, 2004) are all "cooperative" uses of RFID technology. That is, individuals agree to enroll in programs that offer the personal convenience of using RFID and presumably choose when to do so. Similarly, access cards are often a condition of employment as well as an individual convenience, and employees typically know when they are using them. In contrast, objects with RFID tags that come into the possession of retail customers expose those individuals to "uncooperative" reading of the tag, i.e., the tag carried by an individual may be read without that individual knowingly participating in the exchange. (Of course, such uncooperative reading of RFID tags is also possible with access cards, credit card proxies, or toll tags.)

Despite these significant differences, what might be learned from studying access cards? As with other uses of RFID, access cards offer clear benefits to persons and institutions. An access card is arguably more convenient to use than a key and, from an organizational perspective, offers a more cost-effective way to implement physical security. However, these benefits come with a price: Using the device changes an individual's degree of privacy.

In our results we discuss how policy is formulated and explore how sensor data about access card use, linked to individuals, are handled. Explicit or de facto data-handling policies will need to be formulated for all applications that can link sensor data to individuals. Experience with access cards can inform how such policies should be created because access card systems have already grappled with procedures that govern the retention and use of personally identifiable data.

We conducted case studies of six private-sector organizations and their policies for the collection and use of personally identifiable information obtained from access cards. These access cards rely on RFID technology to make them simple and easy to use. RFID tags are usually embedded in small plastic objects that can be attached to key rings, or in a card similar to a credit card. In the latter case, photographs or text can be printed on the card to provide visible information about its bearer. An access card is typically issued to and used by a single individual—like a key—to gain entry to physical facilities (such as a building or a room within a building).

Cards with embedded RFID tags are a simple, easily understood illustration of competing concerns and how such concerns are balanced:

- *The access card provides personal convenience.* It is easier and simpler to carry and use than a physical key—it must merely be waved near a reader.
- *The access card provides security.* Typically, a door lock is controlled by the system reading the access card. The card authorizes access to a controlled location for its bearer, allowing finer-resolution entry controls and making it difficult for those without authorization to enter.
- *The access card reveals otherwise private information about an individual.* It enables the collection of data about each use of the card that can be assembled into a picture of its user's behavior. Unlike a physical key, the access card has a unique identifier that is typically associated with only one person and provides a way for the access control system to observe the behavior of individuals as the cards are used.

Since RFID-based access card technology has been in workplace environments for some time, it provides an opportunity to study policies governing the retention and use of the personally identifiable information it generates. Our approach is a replicated case study to address the following broad questions:

1. Are there common principles underlying private sector privacy policies for data generated by RFID-based access control systems?
2. Are these policies communicated to the employees who use access cards?

We begin our discussion with an overview of privacy in the workplace. We follow that with an explanation of the methodology used. We then present a summary of answers to the research questions provided by our respondents. We close with an analysis and discussion of our findings.

CHAPTER TWO

Privacy In the Workplace

Privacy in the U.S. workplace has few protections. The Electronic Communications Privacy Act of 1986 (ECPA, 86) is a U.S. federal statute that establishes the privacy of employee communications in the workplace. It generally prohibits the interception of electronic communications but specifically allows employers to monitor their networks for business purposes and in particular to monitor communication networks with employee consent—actual or implicit.

These broad exceptions enable employers to monitor all forms of electronic communications in the workplace (e.g., e-mail, instant messaging, voice calls, voice mail), so long as the results of such monitoring are not used to punish labor-organizing activities. This constraint arises from the National Labor Relations Act (NRLA, 1935). Much of the advice available to employees and employers about workplace privacy (e.g., EPIC, 2004; and PR, 2004) concludes that there is very little workplace privacy in the United States.

A review of federal and state privacy statutes (Smith, 2002; Smith, 2004) in the United States does not reveal any legislation specifically dealing with employee monitoring through tracking their use of access cards. However, as noted in PR, 2004, permissible monitoring of the use of employer-supplied computers does enable an employer to keep track of when an employee is at or away from a computer—a rudimentary form of employee tracking.

Although the U.S. legal formulations of privacy allow employers to create employee agreements that effectively eliminate any expectation of privacy, other frameworks exist or have been proposed. European employers are bound by data protection acts that limit the purposes and scope of data collection about employees and limit data retention. A 1996 International Labor Organization code of practice (ILO, 1996) argues that collection and use of data about employees should be consistent with fair information practices (U.S. Department of Health, Education and Welfare, 1973). This includes ensuring that employees are notified about data collection and that the data are used only for the purposes for which they were originally collected. Against this background, we thought it worthwhile to examine emerging U.S. workplace procedures and practices for handling RFID-generated data. The six private-sector enterprises we studied have implemented very similar (explicit or de facto) policies for the retention and use of access control system records. All but one use the personally identifiable data collected by the system to do more than open doors. None of them informs employees about these policies. Hence, our choice of title for this report—*9 to 5: Do You Know If Your Boss Knows Where You Are?*

CHAPTER THREE

Methods

Our approach involves a replicated case study of six organizations. The organizations we chose all have 1,500 or more employees. All are in the private sector. Two are nonprofits, two are high-tech manufacturers, and two are media services firms (content producers).

For each organization, we identified role incumbents responsible in some capacity for the operation of the access control system (e.g., a director of security) and asked them questions about their organization's use of RFID. Our questions covered the following topics:

- Architecture of the RFID-based access control system
- Integration of access control with other systems
- Data collected by the access control system and the linkage of its records to other databases
- Uses of access control system records
- Policies governing the retention and use of access control system records
- Existence of written policy descriptions and their availability to employees
- Role of the access control system policymakers in the organization.

Participating organizations were asked to identify role incumbents with knowledge in these areas to be interviewed. Interviewees were provided with a list of questions in advance (see the appendix). Interviews were conducted either face-to-face or by phone. The interviews were structured by our list of questions and focused on clarifying the interviewees' answers. In some cases, phone or e-mail follow-up discussions were used to amplify initial responses.

We interviewed representatives of the U.S.-based operations of these six organizations. Their responses refer to their U.S.-based workplaces, even though many of these organizations have an international presence. Our interview questions did not explore differences in approach that might characterize an office located outside of the United States. Given that there are significant differences among national protections for workplace privacy, such an exploration would be a valuable extension of our work.

To verify the accuracy of our findings, participants were asked to review a written summary of their interview. Participants were assured confidentiality and were offered draft copies of reports and presentations describing the results of our study to confirm their unidentifiability.

CHAPTER FOUR

What We Found

We begin with a brief discussion of the architecture of the access control systems included in the study. Architecturally, these systems are very similar, although they differ in some technical details. We have abstracted the responses into a single description with only enough detail to understand the answers to our interview questions. We then present in more detail the answers to the remaining study questions provided by the six participating organizations.

Architecture of the RFID Systems Studied

The conceptual elements of the access control systems used by all the organizations in our case studies are illustrated in Figure 1. Each system comprises a number of antennas used to interrogate RFID tags embedded in access cards, electronics for data acquisition and control, the lock or some other physical security feature under the control of the system, network integration of the distributed electronics, and a centralized database that records the details of the use of access cards. After scanning an access card, the system determines whether the card (and corresponding individual) is authorized entry (or exit) and unlocks the barrier (if authorized to do so). A record of that transaction is (optionally) captured in a database. A high-level explanation of the technologies used to implement RFID tags can be found in Want (2004).

Records stored in the database typically include the unique identifier of an access card, the location of the antenna and lock where it was read, and the time and date it was read. By using a concordance that maps unique identifiers of access cards to the names of the individuals who were issued the cards, this data collection can provide a history of an individual's card use. Given a name or person number, transaction records can also be linked to other records about the individual.

The typical access card system provides an interface (not shown in Figure 1) that allows the system operator to activate and deactivate access control cards and to query the database. Generally, the implicit network connecting RFID readers to the database system is logically or physically separated from other workplace networks. The ability to make database queries and perform data extracts is restricted to a small number of authorized individuals by limiting the terminals that can be used to query the database, controlling physical access to those terminals, and authenticating access control system database users. Tamper-resistant auditing of queries and extracts made by user accounts typically provides an additional way to ensure that the records of an access control system are used appropriately.

Figure 1
Elements of a Typical RFID Access Control System

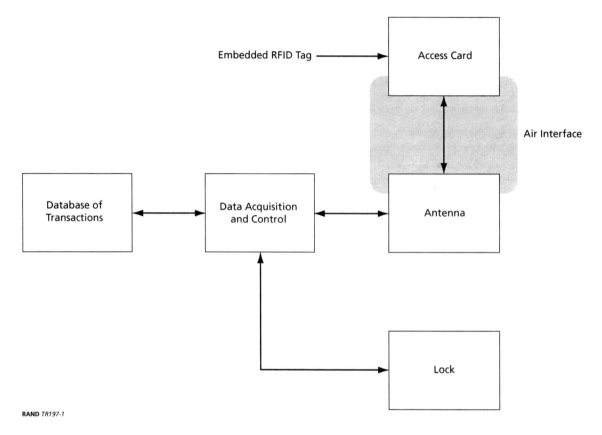

RAND TR197-1

Responses to Interview Questions

System Characteristics

Table 1 summarizes the individual characteristics of the access control systems of the organizations we interviewed. The rows of the table represent the six organizations studied (A through F). The columns characterize their responses to our questions about the scope of the access control system and its relationship to other security systems.

The RFID-based access controls used by the participants in our study are not new systems. They have been in use a minimum of four years (C) and as long as a decade or more (e.g., B). Every system has the capability of recording the unique identity of a card and the time, date, and location of the card's use.

The scope of an access control system can be the entire enterprise (company-wide) or a subset of its facilities. The RFID-based system may be the only way access is controlled (exclusive use), or it may be combined with other access controls, e.g., guarded lobbies that do not require an access card to be scanned by an RFID reader (nonexclusive use). For example, during primary business hours a guard might control employee access to the main entrance of a facility by examining employee credentials (often printed on the access card),

Table 1
RFID Access Control System Characteristics

Case	Category	Years Used	Data Collected	System Scope	Integration with Other Sensors
A	Nonprofit	7	User, time, location	Company-wide, exclusive, external and internal	PIN #; manually with video
B	Nonprofit	15	User, time, location	Company-wide, non-exclusive, external and internal	PIN #, CCTV, alarm systems
C	High-tech manufacturing	4	User, time, location	Company-wide, nonexclusive, external and internal	PIN #, CCTV
D	High-tech manufacturing	7	User, time, location	Company-wide, nonexclusive, external and internal	PIN #, photo ID, CCTV
E	Media services	10	User, time, location	Company-wide, nonexclusive, external and internal	None
F	Media services	8	User, time, location	Company-wide, nonexclusive, external and internal	PIN #, photo ID, CCTV, alarm system

whereas the access control system might be the only access method used during off hours or at other entrances of the same facility. Access cards can be used to control the periphery of an institution's facilities (external control) and/or to limit access to designated areas within a facility (internal control).

All the enterprises we studied use RFID-based access controls throughout the organization both to control peripheral access to facilities and to limit access to designated areas within a facility. Most uses of RFID access cards are nonexclusive—both automated access controls and guards are used to control access in multiple facilities of the organization. Only one organization (A) makes exclusive use of access cards.

Access control systems can be integrated with other systems. For example, doorways and their associated RFID readers are often under the surveillance of a closed-circuit TV (CCTV) camera or video recording system. Typically, data from different systems can be viewed using the same terminal. In some (manual) cases, card transaction data and other data, e.g., a video stream, may need to be viewed at separate terminals.

Access control points may require the bearer of a card additionally to provide a personal identification number (PIN #) for the card to be recognized. This provides verification that the card is in the possession of the person to whom it was issued. PIN numbers are often used to control access to limited areas within an organization (internal access controls), such as a room with sensitive or otherwise highly valuable content.

Access controls can also be integrated with a photo ID system to assist in verification. In this case, the scanning of an access card causes a photo (obtained from an enrollment database indexed by the unique identifier of the access card) to be displayed to a guard who can use it to verify the identity of the bearer of the card.

Finally, access control systems may be integrated with alarm systems so that alarms can be automatically raised via the access control system when unauthorized entry is attempted.

All but one of the participating organizations (E) integrate their access control system with some other system. Manual and automated video systems are common (A, B, C, D, and

F), as are PIN numbers for card verification (A, B, C, D and F). Less common are alarm systems (C and F) and photo ID systems (D and F).

Users and Uses of Data

Data collected by RFID access control systems can be used by multiple parts of an enterprise. An enterprise's security function is the obvious user, but other typical users include line managers and the human resources (HR) and legal departments. Records can be used in ways that personally identify individuals or in aggregate forms that limit the ability to identify individuals. In the latter case, records about multiple individuals are extracted from the database of the access control system, and personally identifying information is removed prior to analysis. In the former case, a typical use might be investigation of asset theft or of compliance with company timekeeping policies. In the case of one respondent (F), record usage also included the investigation of an e-mail threat from an employee's allegedly compromised workstation.

Table 2 shows who uses the data collected by RFID access control systems and in what ways. Security is the primary user. However, the majority of organizations studied also have other users of RFID access control data. These are typically the HR department (A, C, and D), the legal department (C and D), or line management (A, C, and D). Beyond security functions, additional uses rely on both personally identifiable forms of the data and aggregate forms of the data.

Personally identifiable data are typically used to investigate an incident, e.g., theft, or to prove or disprove allegations of employee misconduct (A, B, C, D, and F). Some participants reported that personally identifiable data are also used for public safety, e.g., to account for employees after events that have the potential to harm them or to plan emergency procedures (A and F). In contrast to monitoring individual employee behavior, in one instance (C) personally identifiable data were used to monitor and ensure group compliance with established corporate work rules (e.g., attendance hours) after the acquisition of another company (work culture monitoring). Only one organization (E) limits the use of its RFID access control system to simply controlling access.

Table 2
Users and Uses of the RFID Access Control System Data

Case	Category	Data Users	Individually Identified Data Uses	Aggregate Data Uses
A	Nonprofit	Security, HR, line managers	Individual investigations, public safety	Access logistics
B	Nonprofit	Security	Individual investigations	Logistics; cost analysis
C	High-tech manufacturing	Security, HR, line managers, legal	Individual investigations; work culture monitoring	Government-required logistics
D	High-tech manufacturing	Security, HR, line managers, legal	Individual investigations, location access checks	None
E	Media services	Security	None	None
F	Media services	Security	Individual/threat investigations, personal safety	Security logistics

Aggregate data are used by a majority of the respondents for logistics (A, B, C, and F). Uses ranged from studying arrival and departure patterns (A, B, and F), e.g., to ensure that heavily used entrances had adequate staff or RFID readers to avoid backups at peak hours, to providing government-required information (C)—in this case, to an Air Quality Management District.

Policy and Policymaking

We asked respondents to comment on the following facets of policy related to RFID access control system data: retention of data, auditing practices, publication of policies, policymakers, and allowed linkage to other personally identifiable data. Their responses are summarized in Table 3.

Policies should be developed to govern the use of records collected by access control systems. There are several important policy dimensions. The most obvious is the enforcement of policies governing access to and analysis of the captured records. Policy also requires specification of a data retention interval. Such rules typically require audits to ensure compliance by the organizational units charged with collecting and protecting data assembled by access control systems. These policy choices may or may not be explicitly communicated to the employees who use RFID-based access control systems.

No participating organization has a limited data retention policy. All retain all access control system data indefinitely.

Most of the organizations we studied audit the use of their system records (B, C, D, and F), generally by means of a self-audit. Self-audits are conducted by the organizational unit responsible for operating the access control system.[1] Two organizations do not conduct audits at all (A and E). Only one employs an external auditor (C). The external auditor is not part of the enterprise.

Table 3
Policies Related to RFID Access Control System Data

Case	Category	Data Control	Explicit Policies	Policymaker	Other Database Links
A	Nonprofit	Stored indefinitely, no audits	No	Corporate security	Manually to HR
B	Nonprofit	Stored indefinitely, self-audit	No	Corporate security	Manually to HR
C	High-tech manufacturing	Stored indefinitely, external audit	No	Corporate facilities/ security	HR
D	High-tech manufacturing	Stored indefinitely, self-audit	Yes. Held within security	Corporate security	Manually to HR
E	Media services	Stored indefinitely, no audits	No	Corporate security	Manually to HR
F	Media services	Stored indefinitely, self-audit	No. Operational procedures in security	Facility operations	Medical records/ HR

---

[1] This is in contrast to an internal audit, in which a separate unit of the organization, e.g., Finance, conducts the audit.

Most organizations do not have explicit (written) policies governing the use of RFID access control system records (A, B, C, E, and F). By this, we mean they have no enterprise-wide policy statement explaining the retention, uses, or authorized users of the records collected by the access control system. One company (D) has an explicit policy, but it is not provided to all employees—only to those in the security function of the organization. Another (F) maintains a written set of procedures for operating the access control system. These rules were not described as enterprise-wide policy. Thus, the organizations we studied have no permanent enterprise statement of the rules nor a guarantee that an enterprise-wide process will be used to maintain or change the rules. In our view, therefore, they have no written enterprise-wide policy. Responsibility for creating the policies governing issues such as retention and use of access control system records can reside with the organizational unit operating the system (typically a security function) or can be viewed as an institutional obligation of an officer of the enterprise. In every case we studied, the policymaker is either the security or facilities department. These departments are also responsible for operating the access control system. None of the organizations we studied regarded the policy for access control system data retention and use to be an enterprise-wide policy that should be managed and overseen by an officer of the enterprise (e.g., a vice president).

Last, every organization indicated that the records collected by the access control system were linked (via an employee's name or similar identifier) to other enterprise databases. These linkages always included personnel records (HR) and in one case (F), included medical records. In that instance, the linkage to medical records was used to allow first responders to a medical emergency to scan an employee's badge to call up relevant medical records (e.g., known allergies). The linkage to personnel records is inevitable because individual employees are generally assigned uniquely identified cards, and this concordance needs to be maintained for administrative purposes (e.g., revocation of a lost card). In two cases (C and F), the linkage of access control system records to other records is fully automated.

CHAPTER FIVE

Results

It is quite clear from our six cases that the enterprises studied have many things in common about the way they use access control systems and the data they generate. Several principles stand out:

Linkage of access control system records with other personally identifiable data is commonplace. Access control systems are typically integrated with other forms of surveillance, such as video cameras, and the two sources of surveillance data are routinely linked. Linkage with personnel records is also commonplace. Most surprising was the linkage (albeit in only one case) with medical records.

Linkage with video cameras serves a security need. It is typically used either to verify the identity of the user of an access card (e.g., by displaying an enrollment photo that a monitor can compare to the video image from a remote location) or for forensic purposes (e.g., after a theft of assets).

The linkage of access control system and personnel records is also not surprising because a routine use of RFID access control system records appears to be investigations of misconduct. These are routine in the sense that they are planned although not necessarily frequent. Other routine uses of aggregate data include planning and monitoring, both internal (e.g., flow of employees through an entrance) and external to the enterprise (e.g., reporting attendance information to a regional government for air quality management purposes).

There is a clear public safety motivation for the linkage to medical records and, in this case (F), there is a written policy (developed by the security department) for the use of the access control system data. Nevertheless, linkage with medical records raises additional privacy and operational considerations.

Arguably, these are all legitimate uses of access control system records. In at least two cases (D and F), the rules for use are explicitly defined. Although access control systems provide features that support audits of their use, the majority of audits of compliance with policy are internal ones overseen by the same organizational unit that operates the access control system.

The final principle emerging from our case study sites is that access control system records are retained indefinitely. Our interviews did not explore why there is an apparent reluctance to destroy records after some length of time. Since the data can be used as evidence in criminal investigations and to justify employee sanctions, it may be that enterprises feel compelled to retain them in the event that actions based on the data are appealed.

Although the policies of the cases studied have common features, the employees of the participating enterprises are not likely to know what those policies are. Knowledge of the policies is typically limited to the people and organizational units concerned with security and safety—who also set those policies. Officers of the enterprise are not involved. While the security or facilities departments may report to a corporate officer, we found no evidence that policies, even if made explicit, are seen as the responsibility of an officer or are approved by an officer. Furthermore, corporate officers do not regularly review audits to determine compliance with policies.

Absent enterprise-wide, explicit policies governing the collection, retention, and use of access control system records, our case studies suggest that two implicit principles guide the use of these records. First, security and public safety trump personal privacy. The cases we studied suggest that securing the workplace, investigating instances of theft or misconduct, accounting for employees after emergencies, and providing effective responses to medical problems are the priorities favored in the design and operation of the systems we studied. Second, employment policies trump personal privacy. The case studies suggest that organizations are using access control system data to enforce organizational norms (e.g., compliance with work hours). We encountered uses of access control system data to enforce rules governing employee conduct (A, B, C, D, and F), and to monitor collective behavior (C).

Interestingly, most employees are never informed about these policies, even if they are explicitly documented. Our own experience with RFID-based access cards led us to start casually exploring the policies of the institutions whose RFID cards we use. We found that we did not know, nor could we readily learn, about the policies governing the use of data collected by the access control systems. Furthermore, few of our colleagues had ever thought to ask about applicable policies and certainly did not know what they were. This absence of understanding motivated us to undertake these case studies. If our experiences are representative, we would characterize the "meta" policy about access control system data use in the private sector (and possibly also the public sector) as: "Don't ask, don't tell."[1]

---

[1] This maxim contrasts sharply with explicit and widely disseminated policies about the use of the cards themselves (e.g., "Do not let another person borrow your card," "Do not use your card to let someone else enter the building," "Report lost or stolen cards immediately," and so on).

CHAPTER SIX

Discussion

Recommendations

Based on our case studies, what advice would we offer to an enterprise planning to introduce RFID-based access controls? We think it is important to have an explicit policy for use of data associated with an access control system, based on conscious decisions about how they should and should not be handled.

The advantage of an explicit policy is that the act of creating or revising it provides the impetus to think through the desired organizational response to various situations that might present themselves. Without an explicit plan, an enterprise runs the risk of making policy "on the fly" and under pressure, e.g., when a law enforcement officer requests access to records as part of an investigation that may or may not be initiated by the enterprise. The act of constructing or revising the policy also provides an opportunity to establish limits on the use of the data collected by the system, e.g., a request for their use as evidence in a civil action, such as a divorce proceeding seeking to establish that a spouse was not where he or she claimed to be.

An explicit policy statement further helps to ensure that multiple individuals operating the access control system respond to requests to use its records in a consistent and predictable fashion. It also helps to ensure consistency when responsibility for the operation of the access control system transitions from one individual to another.

What factors should be considered in constructing such a policy? In our view, the factors to consider include the following:

- The scope of the system (i.e., who will be asked to use RFID-based access cards, where, and when)
- The data that will be collected by the system
- What links will be allowed and not allowed between the access control system records and other collections of records (e.g., personnel and medical)
- The policy implications of allowed links
- The retention schedule for access control system records
- Organizational units and role incumbents allowed to request the data, either in individually identifiable or aggregate form

- Who can access the system to provide data for allowed uses (probably not someone in the same organizational unit that makes the request, e.g., HR may request records, but Security provides them without HR ever being able to access the system directly)
- Procedures for approving new (unanticipated) uses of access control system records
- Procedures for providing access control system records in response to requests and/or orders from outside the organization
- Procedures for dealing with unauthorized use of access control records
- The auditing plan.

Who should be accountable for the policy? The scope of the system should determine the answer. If, as in all of our case studies, the scope of the system is the entire enterprise, then the policy is an enterprise policy. An officer of the organization should be accountable for it. If the scope of the system is limited to a department or some other subset of an enterprise, then the individual responsible for the operation of that unit should be accountable for it.

Who should audit compliance with the policy? The auditors of the policy should not be the individuals responsible for running the access control system, especially those individuals authorized to query the collected data. Independent audits provide some assurance that an "insider" has not misused the data and suppressed any record of misuse. Independence might be achieved using in-house auditing services (e.g., the finance unit of the organization), or with an auditor external to the enterprise. The individual who is accountable for the policy should review and accept the results of audits.

What is a reasonable retention policy? In our view, retaining data forever is not a reasonable policy choice. The uses of records allowed by a policy should also serve to set time limits for its applicability and the length of any appeals processes related to those uses.[1] Beyond those limits, there is little value to the data, although the potential for abuse remains.

Should employees be informed about the policy? To the extent that we understand the law, nothing prohibits private-sector enterprises from monitoring employee use of institutional resources, such as phones and e-mail, or compels the enterprise to disclose when it does so. Monitoring and recording employees' use of access cards to enter and/or leave facilities appears to be well within the rights of enterprises. However, nothing prevents them from making their policies known, and fair information practices codes would encourage them to do so.

Are the policies of the six enterprises we studied representative? Clearly, we cannot make any generalizations about enterprises based on six case studies. However, the American Management Association (AMA) has surveyed workplace "e-policies"("2003 E-Mail Rules, Policies and Practices," 2003). The AMA's survey focused on e-mail and not access control systems. It is based on a much larger sample—more than 1100 organizations. The results indicated that "more than half of U.S. companies engage in some form of e-mail monitoring" (52 percent). At least 59 percent of AMA's respondents say "their organization uses some method of enforcement" of e-mail policies, including termination (22 percent). We too found that employees have been sanctioned based on evidence provided by access control records.

---

[1] Retention schedules can also specify that records should be retained for N years or until all contentions and appeals have been resolved. This means that most records could be destroyed after N years.

Seventy-five percent of AMA's respondents report that their "organization has written policies concerning e-mail." Our study suggests that policies concerning access control records are invisible to most employees but are otherwise similar to e-mail monitoring policies. We speculate that the organizations in our study may be reluctant to make security policies visible to all employees because they fear that doing so would weaken security measures or levels of compliance with policies governing the use of cards (e.g., prohibitions on "tailgating" that require everyone to present an access card when passing through a door). Alternatively, the handy analogy of access cards to physical keys may have led them to overlook the need for data-handling policies when the former replaced the latter. We emphasize that we have no data to support our speculations. Our interviews did not explore organizations' rationales for not disclosing policies.

Reality Versus Recommendations

How do our six case studies compare to our recommendations? Only two of the six organizations (D and F) have an explicit statement of policy. We suspect most organizations have very small staffs (one or two people) responsible for operating the RFID access control systems and authorized to use its database. It would be easy to dismiss the overhead of creating an explicit policy as unwarranted given such a small staff. In our view, however, this increases risk to the enterprise of setting an undesirable precedent for the use of data under the pressure of unanticipated circumstances. It also creates the potential for unintended policy changes when responsibility for the operation of an access control system transitions between employees.

Although every enterprise we studied applies RFID technology to the entire organization, responsibility for the policy regarding the records it generates typically lies within the organizational unit operating the access control system—usually Security or Facilities. We suspect that because the overwhelming majority of RFID transactions are never retrieved for further use, few organizations have ever been confronted with issues about their system records that have become visible to a significant number of employees of the enterprise. Thus, it is likely that the officers of the enterprises do not feel the need to own the policies governing the access control system because the policies have no salient enterprise-wide consequences.[2]

Only one of the six organizations (C) externally audits the use of its access control system data. We suspect that because the staff responsible for operating access control systems is typically very small, there is a willingness to trust individuals' judgments. In larger settings, where management may be supervising a large staff, we might expect to find less reliance on personal trust and more acceptance of the need for an independent audit.

None of the participating organizations has limits on the retention of data. We suspect this is the case because the vast majority of transactions are routine, and most enterprises have not experienced serious challenges about their use of access control system records.

Last, none of the organizations participating in our study communicates to its employees that data collected with access cards are used for more than simply controlling locks.

---

[2] Such consequences could be a future well-publicized lawsuit waiting to happen (e.g., one claiming damages from unauthorized use or release of personally identifiable data).

Although we have noted the legality of this behavior, we also observe that under conventional notions of fair information practices (U.S. Department of Health, Education and Welfare, 1973), which might reasonably be expected to apply to the collection of personal information about employees, enterprises should disclose policies to their employees.[3]

Conclusions

Any reader who uses an RFID-based access card ought to be uneasy after seeing these results. We are.

Fair information practices (e.g., Landesberg et al., 1998) argue that employees ought to be informed about uses of access control system records and have the right to inspect and correct records about their activities. None of the enterprises in our study subscribes to these arguments. It also strikes us that implementing traditional fair information practices for access control systems records would be impractical for some situations, such as the individual's ability to correct an erroneous record. Access control systems collect a lot of detailed information about an employee's movements within an enterprise (down to the level of entering particular rooms). While a personal diary might help an employee recall when he or she was at the office, it seems unlikely that anyone maintains diary entries detailed enough to identify movements within a workplace. Would a personal diary provide sufficient evidence to change an automatically collected access control record claimed to be in error, or to add a transaction claimed to be missing? What would motivate an employee to review or correct records? Most likely it would be the occurrence of an incident whose investigation implicates an individual. At that point, after the passage of time, could any employees reconstruct the details of their daily movements to challenge an automated system? Based on these issues, we see the need for a modified notion of fair information practices with regard to this use of RFID technology.

Our sense of unease is similar to the one experienced when public records (e.g., court records) are made available and searchable online—*practical obscurity* is lost (Harmon, 2001). Manual searches are a barrier that provides a degree of privacy about one's public records. The use of automated access and search removes that barrier and the effective privacy it provides. Conventional (anonymous) keys and/or guarded entrances to facilities provide a degree of privacy. It is difficult in those circumstances for anyone to construct a detailed picture of an employee's comings and goings. Individuals would need to be placed under surveillance to track their movements. Without an RFID access control system, this is an expensive manual process supporting the expectation that individuals enjoy a degree of privacy about their everyday movements in the workplace.

RFID-based access cards—and the policies for the collection, retention, and use of records describing employee actions with such cards—change this balance. Everyone is po-

---

[3] The five guiding principles that serve as the foundation of the U.S. Privacy Act, as well as many industry codes of best practices, are: There must be no secret personal data record-keeping system; individuals must be able to discover what personal information is recorded about them and how it is used; individuals must be able to prevent information about them obtained for one purpose from being used or made available for other purposes without their consent; individuals must have a means to correct or amend a record of identifiable information about them; and an organization that creates, maintains, uses, or disseminates records of identifiable personal data must ensure the reliability of the data for their intended use and must take reasonable precautions to prevent their misuse.

tentially under surveillance all the time, since automated searches of the access control system records are easy and practical. Our sense that our privacy is somehow being violated seems to be related to the change in balance brought about by using information technology that in some ways benefits both the employee and employer. Despite our unease about the loss of privacy, access cards clearly have benefits both for individuals and for security and public safety. As we have noted, they secure facilities in much the same way a conventional key would. They are certainly easier to use than a conventional key, particularly if individual areas or rooms within a facility remain locked and require separate keys.

These conflicting needs illustrate the issues that led us to formulate our research ideas for Project Libra (Balkovich, et al., 2004). The research approach we outlined for Project Libra would help to better understand how communities make policy decisions when information technology creates new conflicts between competing needs or upsets an established balance. Our approach would also help to explain how behavior, policy, and technology mutually adapt to one another with usage and experience.

This study has examined how some enterprises have chosen to answer some of these questions. We have not examined the level of employee awareness of RFID-based access cards and systems or their views about appropriate enterprise policies for the data that can be collected when access cards are used. Such a study is an obvious next step.

Appendix: Interview Questions

The following is the protocol for questions that we used to guide interviews in each of the six participating case-study organizations.

General Questions

- Name of organization
- Worldwide size
- Facility size
- Date
- Interviewees' names

Access Control System Questions

- Is there an access control system at your organization?
- How long has it been in use?
- Why was it put into place?
- Was personal convenience/benefit a factor?
- Was individual privacy considered?
- Where is it used?
  - Company wide or specific locations?
  - External access/internal access or both?
- Is it used exclusively?
  - Is facility access only possible via an electronically controlled point?
  - Are access points manned or unmanned?
  - Is secondary authentication required? (PIN numbers, positive photo verification, biometrics?)
- How does the system work?
  - When and how are individuals enrolled in the system and granted facility access?
  - When and how are changes made to individual privileges? By the card owner? By the system operator?
  - Are there procedures to purge access for former users?
  - Who operates the system/has access to it/receives reports from it?
  - Is user change history stored?

— Is system use logged? (i.e., reports)
- Is the system integrated with other corporate systems? (Video surveillance, etc.)
- Is user behavior monitored? (tailgating, swapping IDs, etc.)

Access Control System Technical Questions

- What technology does it use?
- Is the system distributed or centrally operated?
- What information is stored/transmitted?
  — From card to scanner/scanner to card?
  — From remote scanners to host computer?
- If it is RFID:
  — Is the system active/passive?
  — Are cards read-only or read/write?
  — How is card integrity preserved? (uniqueness of IDs)

Access Control Data Questions

- What information is recorded?
- How is it stored? (i.e. anonymously or identifiably)
- Who owns the information/data storage system?
- Where is it stored?
- How long is it kept?
- Who is allowed to look at it, and why?
- How is data accessed?
- What sort of reports can be generated?
- Can it be linked with other individual data? Is it? How?
- Are there backup copies? If yes, what happens to them?
- Are there audit logs of queries to the personally identifiable records? Who has access to audit logs?

Access Control Policy Questions

- Who made the original decision to implement the system?
- Who makes current decisions about the system?
- Who makes decisions about data access?
- How are system procedures documented and promulgated? (Narrowly to system operators, or broadly to the whole organization?)
- Has the system ever been audited?
- If yes, what aspects, and by whom?
- Have access control data been used for more than building access control?
- Can you describe these circumstances?

- How was the information used/channeled in those cases, e.g., were people aware that access control data were the source of information?

Other Questions

- Do you have other corporate systems that record individually identifiable information? (Only new technologies, e.g., e-mail, voice mail, instant messaging, paging, corporate cell phones, web use, etc.)
- Which ones?
- What type of data do they record?
- Are there organization policies about recording/use of this data?
- Has information from any of these systems ever been used for purposes beyond the original intent? Who/what/when/where/why/how?

Next Steps

- Is any relevant new technology or technology integration planned for access control systems?
- Are there any planned or discussed new policies pertaining to personally identifiable data collected by access control systems, or other electronic systems we discussed?

References

"2003 E-Mail Rules, Policies and Practices" (2003). Online at http://www2.amanet.org/research/pdfs/Email_Policies_Practices.pdf (accessed 2 June 2004).

"2004 RFID Legislation" (2004). Online at http://www.retail-leaders.org/content/default.asp?dbid=483 (accessed 25 May 2004).

"About EPCGlobal Inc." (2003). Online at http://www.epcglobalinc.org/about/about.html (accessed 25 August 2004).

Albrecht, Katherine (2002). "Supermarket Cards: The Tip of the Retail Surveillance Iceberg," *Denver University Law Review,* Vol. 79, No. 4, pp. 534–539, 558–565.

Albrecht, Katherine (2003). "RFID Right to Know Act of 2003: Proposed Legislation to Mandate Labeling of RFID-Enabled Products and Consumer Privacy Protections." Online at www.nocards.org/rfid/rfidbill.shtml (accessed 11 August, 2004).

Balkovich, Edward, Tora Bikson, David Farber, Robert Kraut, James Morris, Peter Shane, and Joel Smith (2004). *Project Libra: Optimizing Individual & Public Interests in Information Technology,* Santa Monica, Calif.: RAND Corporation. Online at http://www.rand.org/publications/CP/CP477/CP477.pdf (accessed November 3, 2004).

Covert, James (2004). "Business Solutions; Down, but Far From Out: RFID Technology is Off to a Disappointing Start; But Retailers are Convinced Its Future is as Bright as Ever," *The Wall Street Journal,* 12 January, p. R.5.

ECPA (1986). *Electronic Communications Privacy Act of 1986.* Public Law 99-508. Washington, D.C.: United States Congress, October 21.

EPIC (2004). "Workplace Privacy," *Electronic Privacy Information Center.* Available at http://www.epic.org/privacy/workplace (accessed 26 July 2004).

Exxon Mobil Oil Corporation (2003). "Speedpass News," Exxon Mobil Oil Corporation. Online at www.speedpass.com (accessed 22 August, 2003).

Feder, Barnaby J. (2003). "Wal-Mart Plan Could Cost Suppliers Millions," *The New York Times,* 10 November, p. C.2.

Harmon, Amy (2001). "As Public Records Go Online, Some Say They're Too Public," *The New York Times,* 24 August, p. A.1.

Henry, Shannon (2003). "Pentagon Boosts High-Tech Tagging," *The Washington Post,* 18 December, p. E1.

ILO (1997). *Protection of Workers' Personal Data: An ILO Code of Practice,* International Labor Organization, Geneva: 1997. Online at http://www.ilo.org/public/english/protection/safework/cops/english/download/e000011.pdf (accessed 30 August 2004).

Landesberg, Martha K., Toby Milgrom Levin, Caroline G. Curtin, and Ori Lev (1998). *Privacy Online: A Report to Congress,* Washington, D.C.: Federal Trade Commission.

Leahy, Patrick (2004). "The Dawn of Micro Monitoring: Its Promise, and Its Challenges to Privacy and Security," *Video Surveillance: Legal and Technological Challenges,* Washington, D.C.: Georgetown University Law Center, 23 March.

NRLA (1935). National Labor Relations Act. 29 U.S.C. §§ 151-169. Title 29, Chapter 7, Subchapter II, United States Code.

New Jersey Department of Transportation (2004). "Welcome to E-Zpass," New Jersey Department of Transportation. Online at www.ezpass.com (accessed 11 August 2004).

PR (2002). "Employee Monitoring: Is There Privacy in the Workplace?" *Fact Sheet 7: Workplace Privacy,* September. Online at http://www.privacyrights.org/fs/fs7-work.htm (accessed 26 July 2004).

_____ (2003). *RFID Position Statement of Consumer Privacy and Civil Liberties Organizations,* Nov. 20. Online at http://www.privacyrights.org/ar/RFIDposition.htm (accessed 30 August 2004).

RFID Journal (2002a). "Special Report Part 6: Improving Logistics," 18 November. Online at www.rfidjournal.com/article/articleview/201/1/5/ (accessed 11 August 2004).

_____ (2001b). "Special Report Part 5: Warehousing Efficiencies," *RFID Journal,* 14 October. Online at www.rfidjournal.com/article/articleview/200/1/5/ (accessed 11 August 2004).

Schwartz, Ephraim (2004). "Siemens to Pilot RFID Bracelets for Health Care," *InfoWorld,* 23 July. Online at www.infoworld.com/article/04/07/23/HNrfidimplants_1.html (accessed 11 August 2004).

Smith, Robert Ellis (2004). *Compilation of State and Federal Privacy Laws,* 2004 Supplement 7-3, Providence, R.I.: Privacy Journal.

_____(2002). *Compilation of State and Federal Privacy Laws,* 2002 Edition, Providence, R.I.: Privacy Journal.

U.S. Department of Health, Education and Welfare, Advisory Committee on Automated Personnel Data Systems (1973). *Records, Computers and the Rights of Citizens,* Washington D.C.: July.

Want, Roy (2004). "RFID: A Key to Automating Everything," *Scientific American,* January, pp. 56–65.

Weissert, Will (2004). "Mexican Attorney General Personally Goes High-Tech for Security," Associated Press, 14 July. Online at apnews.myway.com/article/20040714/D83QQBP80.html (accessed 11 August, 2004).